Cover art and Design: "Helping Hands" by "Andreus" at DepositPhotos.com
Illustrated by: Dolores Melgar
Interior Graphic Art by: Iqoncept, Alexmillos, Pixelsaway, Yurizap & Kikkerdirk at DepositPhotos.com

All rights reserved. No part of this book may be used, reproduced or stored in a retrieval system, or transmitted in any form or by any means, electronic, mechanical, photocopy, recording, or any other, without prior written permission from the publisher, Christina N. Smith, except for brief quotations embodied in critical articles and/or printed reviews.

Publisher's Cataloging-in-Publication data

Names: Smith, Christina Nicole, author | Melgar, Delores, illustrator.
Title: Joseph's journey : when Dad left and never came back / by Christina Nicole Smith ; illustrations by Dolores Melgar.
Description: 2nd edition | Modesto, CA: Be a Blessing Enterprises, 2016.
Identifiers: ISBN 978-0-9981281-0-8 (Hardcover) | 978-0-9981281-1-5 (pbk.) | 978-0-9981281-3-9 (ebook) | LCCN 2016909316.
Summary: When Joseph's father stops coming to visit, his mother takes the opportunity to explain to him about choices.
Subjects: LCSH Children of single parents--Juvenile literature. | Fathers--Juvenile literature. | Mothers and sons--Juvenile literature. | Single mothers--Juvenile literature. | Paternal deprivation--Juvenile literature. | Choice (Psychology) in children--Juvenile literature. | BISAC JUVENILE NONFICTION / Family / Parents | JUVENILE NONFICTION / Social Topics/ Emotions & Feelings | JUVENILE NONFICTION / Social Topics / Self-Esteem & Self-Reliance
Classification: LCC HQ777.4 S65 2016 | DDC 649/.132--dc23

As a mother, how do you explain an absentee father to your child without blame, anger or resentment? Empower them! Seven-year-old Joseph shares his story about when he first learns about the POWER of choice he possesses after his father leaves and doesn't come back. His mother teaches him the difference between *his father's* choices and *his own*. Do Joseph and Mom become angry with Joseph's father? *Well,* a belief is just a thought you keep thinking over and over...find out what happens on Joseph's Journey!

PRINTED IN THE UNITED STATES OF AMERICA

For Information regarding permission contact:

Be A Blessing Enterprises
510.868.2860 ex. 1
email: cnsmithauthor@gmail.com
website: CnSmithAuthor.Com

Dedication

I want to dedicate this book to my parents, Cleveland and Cheryl Smith. My parents were married for 40+ years. "Joseph's Journey" is about how to empower a child in the explaining of an absentee father, however, my father was always there for me until his last breath August 14, 2015. To my brother & sister, we make a great team. Thank you!

To my mentor, George Ramirez, thank you for seeing beyond what I could see and believing in me!
To Iris Nelson & my sister Angela Smith, thank you. I am reborn through the power of breath. To Tambra Harck—thank you for helping me to LIVE MY YUM!

It truly does take a village to raise a child. I want to thank all of those positive individuals in my life that have supported me and my son and our growth. It means a lot-YOU mean a lot. Michael Evans, Hana Nour, James McNeal, Sylvester Griffin, Stephanie Beeby, Stephanie Boone, Jim Noll, Rick Jones, Cedric Jones, Shawn Jones, Margi Myers, Nela Brown, Bernadet Betyaghoub, Debbie Whitten and Evelyn Green.

To Pastor James Long and my Pastor Cousins Mark & Cindy Shephard thank you for baptizing my spirit and dedicating Joseph to the Creator.

**To all the fathers who are absent in their children's lives because they feel there is no other option and no other way but the way they have chosen—

The <u>only</u> one who can limit your possibilities is YOU.
— Jon Gordon

"Don't be afraid to be amazing!"
— Andy Offutt Irwin

Joseph's Journey:
When Dad Left and Never Came Back ©

By Christina Nicole Smith

Illustrations by Dolores Melgar

"A grudge is too heavy for an angel to carry."

—Author Unknown

Hi. My name is Joseph and I want to share my story with you about when I first learned about making choices.

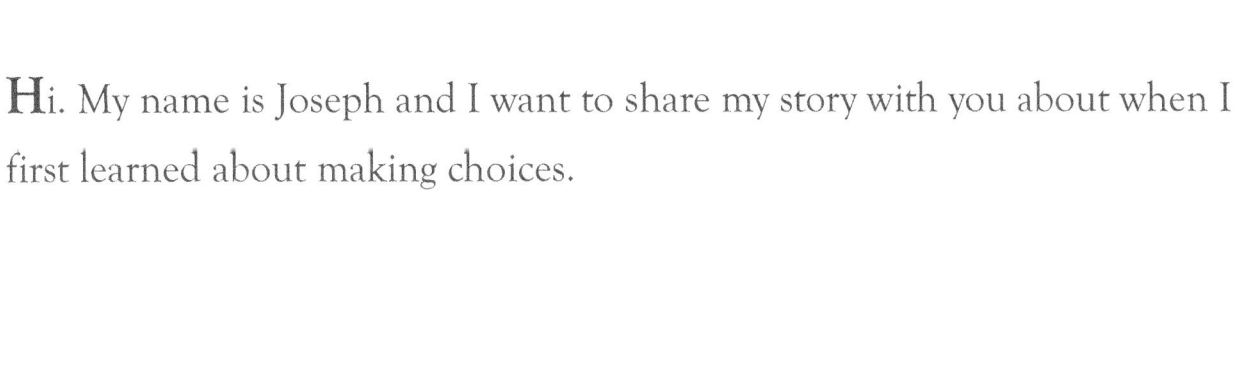

*There are no mistakes in this illustration! The poster messages are blurred for a reason. You must go on a "journey" with Joseph until the end to discover what these messages say.

I wish you love, light, self-growth, acceptance and clarity during your journey. —*Author*

For instance, sometimes your mom might ask you if you want milk, water or juice to drink.

Your choice may be water.

Or your mom may ask you if you want to go to the store with her or if you want to stay home with your grandparents.

You may choose to go with your mom to the store as your choice.

My mom first told me about making choices one day when I asked her where my dad was.* I used to see him at least once a week or every two weeks.

Then, I didn't see or hear from him at all. I didn't know why he didn't come to our house anymore. All I knew was that I felt sad and sometimes angry because I didn't see him anymore.

*Joseph asks: "Where is Dad? Is he going to come over?
*Mom states: "I don't know where Dad is and he doesn't have a phone so I can't call him."

I asked my mom where he was and if she could call him so he could come play with me.

She sighed, "Joseph, I don't know where your dad is and he does not have a phone so I can't call him."

I know mommy loves me and always tells me the truth, so I believe her.

It's just that it seems as if there is nothing I can do except feel sad and angry.

He does not call or come. I don't know what to do!

"Joseph, I want to tell you something," mommy said as she gently took my hands to hold them in hers.

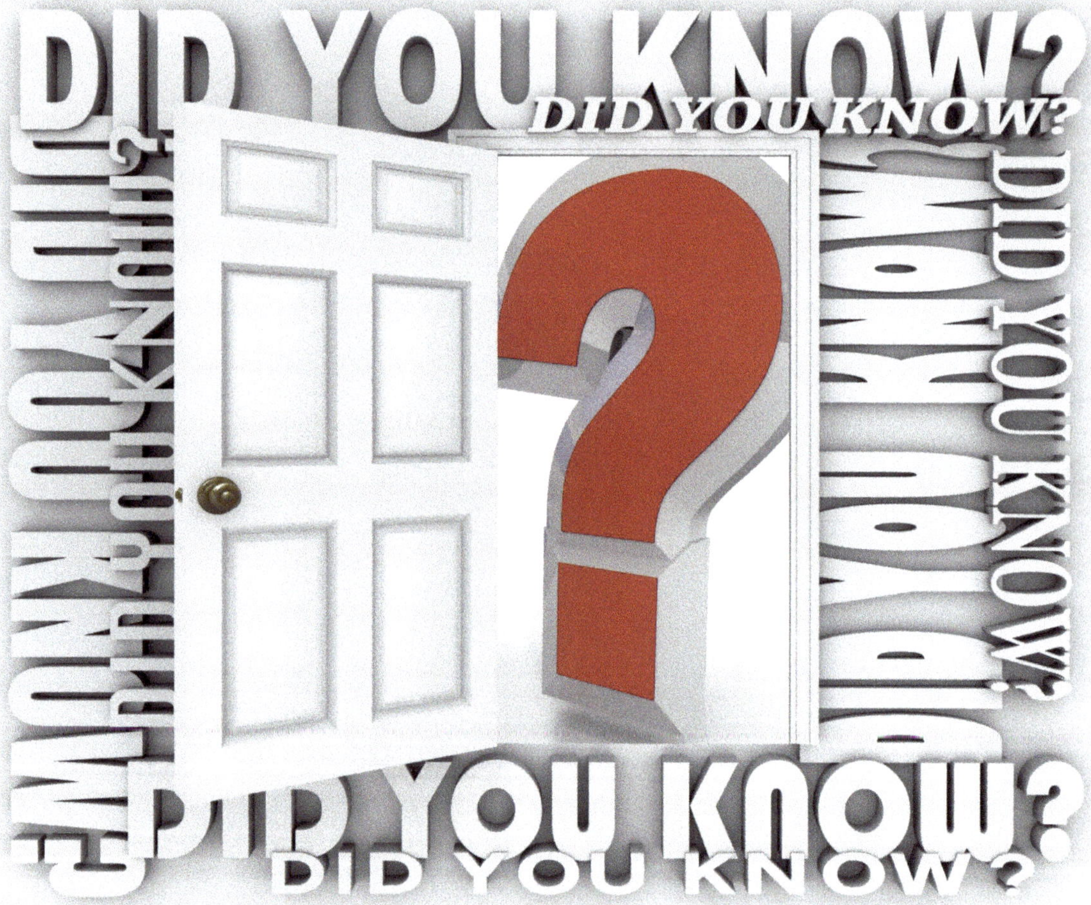
DID YOU KNOW?
DID YOU KNOW?
DID YOU KNOW?
DID YOU KNOW?
DID YOU KNOW?
DID YOU KNOW?
DID YOU KNOW?
DID YOU KNOW?

"**I** know that you miss your daddy and that may make you feel sad. But did you know you have the power to choose the way you want to feel at any time? Everybody has that power. The power to make their own choices.

We are making choices all the time. When I ask you if you want milk, water or juice, you make your choice based on what you like, what you feel you want at the time and what will make you feel good on the inside, right?"

Yes.

"So let's say you choose the milk and you know that is what you want. Then I will be unable to convince you to choose something else.

Even if I say, Joseph no, you do not want the milk. You will say, 'No mommy! I want milk because I like it!'

This is because you know what you want, you know how you feel, and you believe that you are making the best choice for yourself."

"Now, let's talk about your dad's choices. Your dad has his own heart and mind too, right?"**

Yes.

"Everybody does. Your dad makes choices based on what he believes is the best choice for him at the time. We may not understand why. But, we do understand he is using his power to make his OWN CHOICES, right?"

Joseph's word cloud: I can make up my own mind mom. I choose milk. It's my favorite drink!
Dad's word cloud: I have my own mind too and make choices like you son. Everybody else does also. It is a part of life.

So he's choosing not to come over here? Why?

"Yes, he's choosing not to come over here, but I don't know why. Remember, we can't control what your dad does. We can't force him or anyone to do anything. He is your dad, but he is also an individual person. He has the power to make his own choices and control his own actions. Sometimes we will not always understand why some people make the choices they do."

But he's my dad.

"I know dear. Let me give you another example about choices. If another kid hit you, what would you do?"

I don't know.

"Well, you could tell an adult what happened and ask for help, or you could walk away. You could even say something nice to the kid like, 'I don't understand why you hit me, but I choose to forgive you.' There's lots of choices to choose from and you have the power to choose what is best for you.

So let's talk about your dad again. Since we haven't talked to him in awhile, all we know for sure is he is using his Power to Choose not to come here. We don't know the reasons why, but do we let *HIS* CHOICES make us feel bad about ourselves?"

No.

"You can choose to say to yourself, My dad is his own person and he is using his own power to choose. I may not like that he chooses to not come and see me as much as he used to do, but I don't blame myself for the choices my daddy chooses. I have the POWER TO CHOOSE MY OWN THOUGHTS.

So, if you are feeling sad, you can say to yourself, I am finished feeling sad now. I choose to be happy because I can!"

I like that mommy, I didn't know what to do and now I know I have the power to do something about how I feel!

"Remember, NOBODY can MAKE YOU FEEL ANYTHING.

You have YOUR OWN MIND and you're in control of it. So if you're feeling sad, it's because you're choosing it. If you're feeling happy, it's because you're choosing it."

Does your body feel better on the inside when you say you're happy or sad?"

Happy!

"Me Too!"

"Choosing to be happy even when your dad chooses not to come over by himself to spend one on one time with you does not mean that you don't love him and he doesn't love you.

It means that you are CHOOSING to believe what is true for you in your heart, no matter what ANYONE ELSE MAY THINK, SAY, OR DO."

"Do you believe your daddy loves you?"

I do.

"Well then hold onto that dear. Now you are using your power son! Your POWER TO CHOOSE! Joseph, when you get really good at choosing happiness, joy and thankfulness in ANY situation…it will become as easy and fun as laughing, running and jumping!"

Yeah! Mommy?

"Yes Honey?"

Can I have a snack?

"Yes, dear. Do you know what you just did? You just chose to make mommy laugh! Thank you Joseph! I love you son."

Love you too mommy.

And that's how I learned about the POWER in making my OWN CHOICES. Would you like to give it a try?

If you haven't seen your mommy or daddy in awhile, it's okay. You can still have lots of fun in life, be happy, and feel good on the inside because you have the POWER TO CHOOSE.

I still get sad sometimes, it happens. But when it does, I start thinking about all the things that I say thank you for like my toys, my games, yummy snacks, going fun places with my family and then what I felt sad about, goes away because I am choosing happiness. I like that feeling a lot better!

Hey, me and you—we're winners! Don't you ever forget that okay?

Your Friend,

Joseph

P.S. Thank the person that got you this book! They just wanted to help you, like I did, by sharing my story.**

**Remember at the beginning of the book, the images & words were blurred out? Can you read the messages now? Poster #1 states: "I love myself." Poster #2 asks: "What am I grateful for today?"

Hopefully, after going on this "journey" with Joseph, you feel that you have learned new ways of thinking that will serve your highest good and help you to soothe yourself in those times you may feel sad. What are you grateful for today? —Author

THE END

ABOUT THE AUTHOR

Whenever Joseph says he is scared about one thing or another, I will always ask him, "What does Louise Hay say?" Then he will recall, "Sometimes we all get scared, but we can do it anyway!"

I had reservations about sharing "our story" with others at first because I am a private person. However, it appears that now, more than ever, this message of empowerment and healing needs to reach many people. So I took Louise's advice!

May you find comfort in these words and may this message open the door to a path of love, compassion, grace and healing.

At the present time, I am continuing my journey of healing and self-growth, choosing to make the best of each moment as it is. The more I talk about "this" in a positive light, the better I feel and the stronger I become. It wasn't possible to bottle this feeling of empowerment and give it to others, so I wrote "Joseph's Journey" instead!

"Joseph's Journey" is Christina Smith's first children's book. She currently lives in California with her immediate family. Joseph is taking piano lessons, practicing martial arts and also coming into his own as a writer. His poetry has been published in two compilation books through the America Library of Poetry in 2014 & 2015. He is also continuing his journey of self-growth and awareness.

Acknowledgement

To Louise L. Hay, your teachings have inspired me to write this book and share my story with the world. Sharing who you are has helped me to become a better woman, mother and to truly lead by example by walking the "talk".

This is the lesson I have learned and now share with others through Joseph's Journey:

"I allow others to be themselves...
I cannot force others to change. I can offer them a positive mental atmosphere where they have the possibility to change if they wish, but I cannot do it *for* or *to* other people. Each person is here to work out his or her own lessons and if I fix it for them, then they will just go and do it again because they have not worked out what they needed to do for themselves. All I can do is love them, allow them to be who they are and know that the truth is always within them and that they can change at any moment they want." —

Excerpt from:
Inner Wisdom:
Meditations for the Heart and Soul
by Louise L. Hay

"*Our emotional reality is ultimately our own responsibility. We can <u>decide</u> to bless someone, even if we don't like his or her behavior, and in doing so we're freed from the limited vision by which we judged him or her to begin with. It's our willingness to see the innocence in someone, even when they have shown us their guilt, that gives us the capacity to transform both their experience and our own.*

While we are born with a perfect capacity to love, each of us is tempted by the realities of life to withhold our love and defend against pain. Compassion, defenselessness, and unconditional love are much easier to express before we become aware of how dangerous life and love can be. Only very small children—and saints—are really good at it."

Excerpt from "Everyday Grace"—

by Marianne Williamson

If you enjoyed "Joseph's Journey", please rate & review it. When you take the time to write an honest review, it lets others know that you read something worthwhile and they might consider doing the same.

As an independent publisher, there isn't a marketing budget to reach the folks who may genuinely want to have access to a book like this. So taking the time to write an honest review on Amazon, iTunes, Barnes & Noble, Kobo, Google Books, or Goodreads would be received as a truly meaningful gift from you that would sincerely be appreciated!

Sending waves of gratitude and abundance your direction!

Joseph's Journey:
When Dad Left and Never Came Back ©

Available from Amazon.com and other online stores

Want to talk more? You can find me here:

https://www.goodreads.com/cnsmithauthor1

https://twitter.com/cnsmithauthor

https://www.linkedin.com/in/christinanicolesmit

https://cnsmithauthor.com

Channel Name: CNSMITH AUTHOR

www.ingramcontent.com/pod-product-compliance
Lightning Source LLC
Chambersburg PA
CBHW061931290426
44113CB00024B/2876

This Book Belongs To: ....

Blacks Publishing

Published by Blacks Publishing Ltd

First published in the UK 2015

Copyright © Blacks Publishing Ltd

All rights reserved.

"The Lorikeet" and The Lorikeet logo are trademarks of Blacks Publishing and are used under license. Logo copyright @ Blacks Publishing

Blacks Publishing Limited Reg. No. 9250806

Printed in Great Britain

www.blackspublishing.com

Carey:

Dedicated to my amazing mother Margaret Johnson, grandmother Verna Edie and brothers Kurtis and Ezra Johnson I love you loads x

Kia:

To Mum and Nan eternally grateful x

Meet The Lorikeet

He has bright colourful feathers like a rainbow
He loves playing with his friends
And really loves adventures!
Come and join The Lorikeet on an adventure!

Flip to the back for fun and colouring pages

Written and Illustrated by Carey Black & Kia Mills

It is breakfast time in the rainforest.

The Lorikeet is hungry and wants fruit for breakfast.

Normally he would eat a rosy **red** or crunchy **green** apple,

but today he wants to try something new.

So off he goes into the rainforest with a Keet-Keet-Ka-Keet!

The Lorikeet comes across his friend Ant. Ant is trying to find food for him and his family. His favourite foods are crispy **green** leaves. Today is his lucky day! He finds the **greenest**, freshest, crunchiest leaf he has ever seen. The only problem is, the leaf is trapped under a BIG rock.

Ant tried pulling, pushing and lifting the rock but nothing he tried worked. The rock was just too heavy. The proud Ant tired himself out and was all out of ideas. He is still young and maybe not as strong as he thinks he is.

Luckily the Lorikeet was there to help.

He picked up the rock with his beak and threw it far away.

Ant was so happy. "Thanks Lori" said Ant. "I could not have done it without you. Why don't you join me and my family for breakfast?"

The leaves sounded tasty but this is not what the Lorikeet had in mind. As he flew away he squawked. "Thank you Ant but not today, something else might come my way."

The Lorikeet travelled deeper into the rainforest.

He finds his friend Monkey staring high up in to the trees at a large bunch of bananas. It looks like Monkey is hungry too.

Monkey's favourite food to eat is ripe yellow bananas.

"Why don't you climb the tree to reach them?" The Lorikeet asked.

With a big sigh Monkey tells the Lorikeet that he doesn't know how, he was very embarrassed can you imagine a Monkey that cannot climb trees?

The Lorikeet watched as his friend tried to climb the banana tree again and again........and again. Sadly the poor Monkey would feel dizzy, lose balance and crash to the ground.

"Don't look down Monkey, that is why you are dizzy. Monkeys are born to climb trees, so believe in yourself!" The Lorikeet said.

So the nervous Monkey tried again branch by branch, before he knew it he was at the top of the tree.

"Well done Monkey" cheered the Lorikeet.

With a big bunch of bananas the happy Monkey offered to share his fruit.

"Thank you Monkey but not today, something else might come my way." Said the Lorikeet as he waves goodbye.

The hungry Lorikeet finds another friend in the rainforest. This time he comes across Jaguar, she is also looking for breakfast.

Her favourite foods to eat are berries but she likes the juicy **blueberries** the most.

"Why do you look so confused Jaguar?" The Lorikeet asked. "I am confused because I am colour blind", Jaguar replied. This means it is hard for her to see colours. "So I can not tell which are the **blueberries**."

"This is a rhyme my dad taught me about **blueberries**"

says the Lorikeet.

"If it smells sweet, it's good to eat,
if it does not then please stop"

The **blue** smell sweet, the **red** smell of feet,
the **purple** smell sour, the **black** smell of flowers,
the **green** smell minty and the **yellow** smell stinky.

"Now I will always know which berries are **blue**." Would you like to try some"? Jaguar asked. The Lorikeet not hungry for berries smiles and says "Thank you Jaguar but not today, something else might come my way".

Still very hungry and with a grumbling tummy.

The Lorikeet thinks about all the tasty food he could have eaten.

He could have had crispy **green** leaves with Ant, ripe **yellow** bananas with Monkey or juicy **blueberries** with Jaguar.

"**Grrrrrrr**" the Lorikeets belly growls louder and louder and he wonders if he made a mistake not sharing with his friends.

Then he sees it! A fresh **brown** coconut high in trees. The Lorikeet now knows what he wants and it looked delicious! He has never tasted a coconut before.

He flew up the tree and pecked one off the branch.

It fell to the ground but the leaves on the floor were so soft the coconut did not crack open.

A tear rolled down the Lorikeets face, he had no idea how to open its thick shell and was getting very hungry.

Just then...

"WE'LL HELP YOU!" Three voices screamed.

Out of nowhere it was Ant, Monkey and Jaguar to the rescue.

Monkey picked up the coconut and climbed the tree.

Ant with his family members carried the big rock under the tree.

Then Monkey dropped the coconut onto the rock, it cracked open

and Jaguar cut it up into little pieces

with her sharp claws for the Lorikeet to eat.

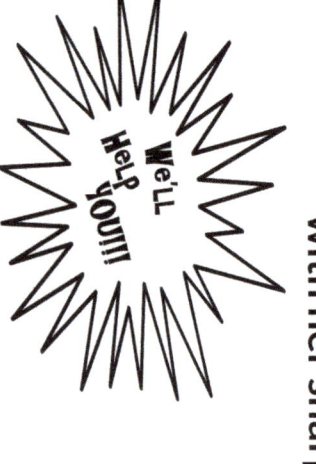

It was just then the Lorikeet realised how lucky he was to have such great friends. He also learnt that it is very important to help a friend in need.

No matter how big or small the problem may be.

So after an adventurous morning, The Lorikeet finally gets to enjoy his new favourite fruit with all his friends.

The End*

Lorikeet Lessons

- A Lorikeet is a small or medium sized Parrot?
- Lorikeets are known for their colourful feathers and when they stick out their tongues it's furry just like a brush
- Lorikeets also like to eat nectar off of different blossoms and fruits
- They are mainly found in rainforests

- In the rainforest you can find up to half of all the animals and plants on the planet

- Ants are really strong they can lift up to 5000 times their body weight!

- Monkeys don't eat banana peels just like humans

- The spots on a Jaguars body are called rosettes because they look like roses

- Please Remember. Never eat any fruit you find like The Lorikeet and friends, always make sure to get permission from a parent or guardian first!!!

The Lorikeet

More books to look out for

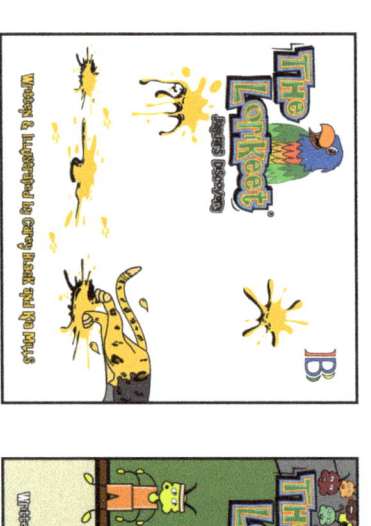
Jaguar's Discovery

Antlympics

Are Monsters Real?

Even more fun and games at www.thelorikeet.co.uk

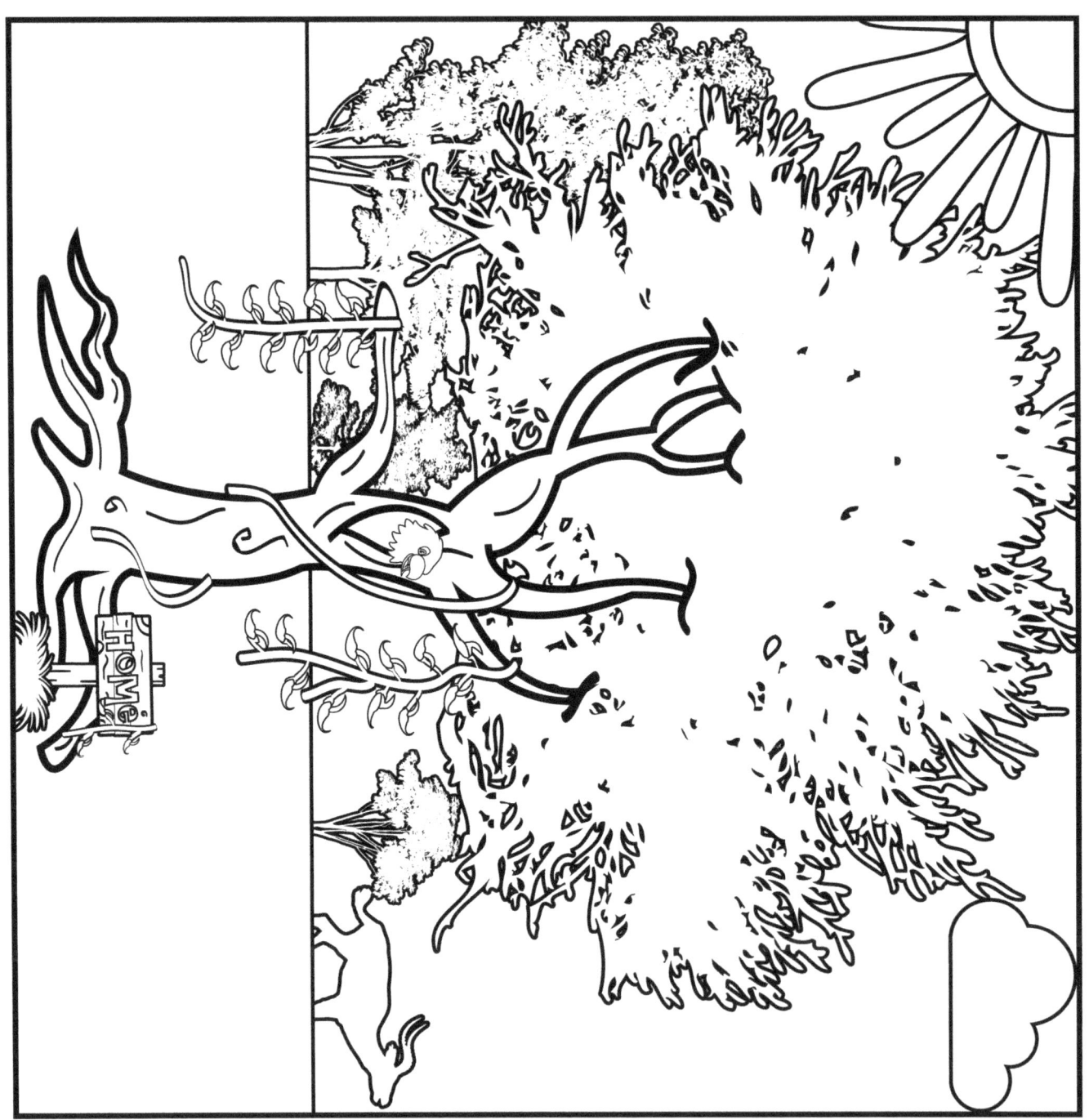

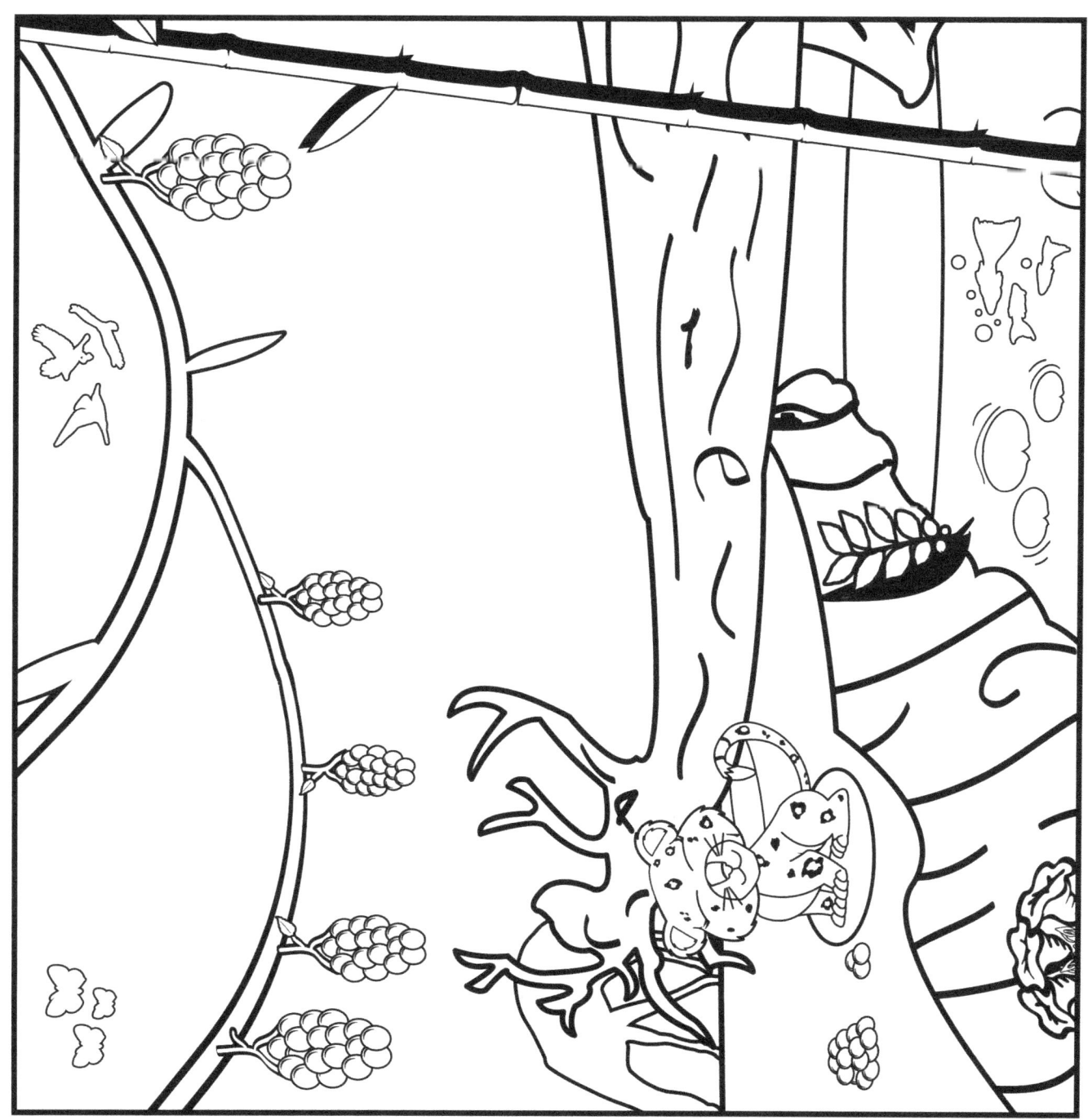

Spot the Difference

The are 5 differences between the pictures, can you spot them all??

Answers:
a) Coconut on monkeys head
b) Dragonfly in top right
c) Part of the sun is missing
d) Tree missing in background
e) Coconut piece The Lorikeet is going to eat

www.ingramcontent.com/pod-product-compliance
Lightning Source LLC
Chambersburg PA
CBHW061931290426
44113CB00024B/2872